Network
Trace Analysis
Pattern-Oriented

Version 1.0

Dmitry Vostokov
Software Diagnostics Services

Published by OpenTask, Republic of Ireland

OpenTask books and magazines are available through booksellers and distributors worldwide. For further information or comments send requests to press@opentask.com.

A CIP catalogue record for this book is available from the British Library.

ISBN-l3: 978-1-908043-58-0 (Paperback)

First printing, 2013

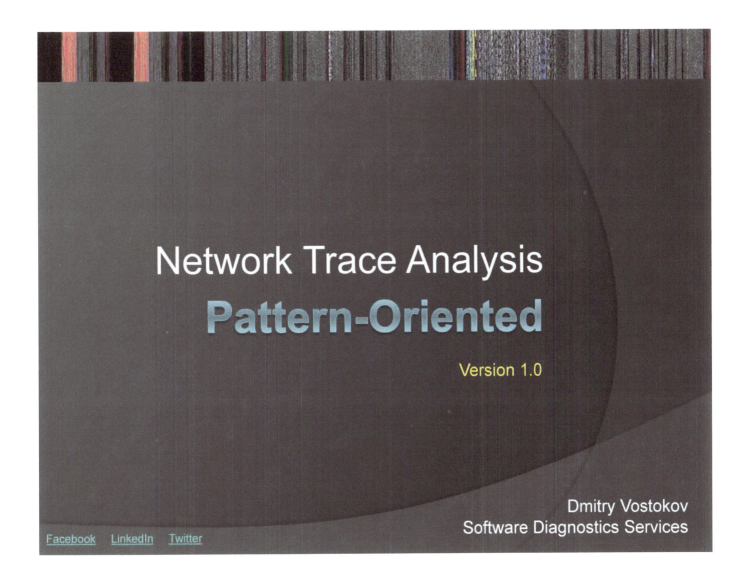

Hello Everyone, my name is Dmitry Vostokov and I introduce today a software narratological approach to network trace analysis. I decided to keep this presentation short and as simple as possible. If anything needs to be added or modified in the future I create another version of it.

Facebook:
http://www.facebook.com/SoftwareDiagnosticsServices

Linkedin:
http://www.linkedin.com/company/software-diagnostics-services

Twitter:
http://twitter.com/DumpAnalysis

Wireshark

Hark

- Listen (to) *"Hark! There's the big bombardment."*
- Speak in one's ear; whisper

Shorter Oxford English Dictionary

Hark back *(idiom)*

- To return to a previous point, as in a narrative

http://www.thefreedictionary.com/hark

Before we start I'd like to offer an interpretation of Wireshark tool pronunciation. You see that it is connected with a notion of a narrative, a story. Why a narrative you see during this presentation.

Prerequisites

⊚ Interest in software diagnostics, troubleshooting, debugging and network trace analysis

⊚ Experience in network trace analysis using Wireshark or Network Monitor

Prerequisites for this presentation are very simple and I suppose you all like me enjoy diagnosing software problems and often going side-by-side network problems. I also assume that you already have experience in network trace analysis or at least familiarity with Wireshark interface. In such a case I hope this webinar outlines a unified pattern-oriented approach to network trace analysis in the context of general software trace analysis. If you only have experience in software log analysis but don't have any experience in network trace analysis it should provide a foundation for further study. A separate training course is coming soon too that will cover much more with detailed exercises. Originally I planned to add some demonstrations too but due to the time limit and size of this presentation (it grew up to almost 50 slides) I decided to omit them.

Why?

- A common diagnostics language

- Network diagnostics as software diagnostics

Why we advocate a general pattern approach to traditional network trace analysis? Because we need a unified language in the context of general software diagnostics and network trace analysis is largely a part of software diagnostics. As we would see later network trace structure and dynamics are similar to general software logs, for example, from Windows Process Monitor or from large scale software systems such as Citrix products which have their own tracing infrastructure based on Event Tracing for Windows.

Software Diagnostics

A discipline studying abnormal software structure and behavior in software execution artifacts (such as memory dumps, software and network traces and logs) using pattern-driven, systemic and pattern-based analysis methodologies.

© 2013 Software Diagnostics Services

First, I would like to remind you a definition of software diagnostics we put forward in one of our previous webinars. So you see that network trace analysis and associated software behavior fall under our definition of software diagnostics.

Pattern-driven:
http://www.patterndiagnostics.com/Introduction-Software-Diagnostics-materials

Systemic:
http://www.patterndiagnostics.com/systemic-diagnostics-materials

Pattern-based:
http://www.dumpanalysis.org/pattern-based-software-diagnostics

Diagnostics Pattern

> A common recurrent identifiable problem together with **a set of recommendations** and **possible** solutions to apply in a specific context.

Next we would like to mention a definition of a software diagnostics pattern. There are some differences with a usual definition of a pattern from software construction such as architectural and design patterns. The difference is that often upon a diagnostic encounter we provide recommendations and possible solutions instead of just problem solutions. Recommendations may include immediate actions, for example, upon the detection of a significant amount of network traffic.

Pattern Orientation

Pattern-driven

- Finding patterns in software artefacts
- Using checklists and pattern catalogs

Pattern-based

- Pattern catalog evolution
- Catalog packaging and delivery

So you see that software diagnostics is about patterns and pattern recognition. Let's say it is pattern-oriented and includes pattern-based and pattern-driven parts. Pattern-driven is about diagnostics process and pattern-based is about pattern life cycle. We first start with the pattern-driven part.

Catalog Classification

⊚ **By abstraction**

Meta-patterns

⊚ **By artifact type**

Software Log*   Memory Dump   **Network Trace***

⊚ **By story type**

Problem Description   Software Disruption   UI Problem

⊚ **By intention**

Malware

In pattern-driven analysis we use pattern catalogs of pattern descriptions. Catalogs can be classified by abstraction, for example, as software diagnostics meta-patterns which are patterns of software diagnostics itself, by the type of software execution artifacts, such as software traces and logs, memory dumps and network traces, by story type, such as by problem descriptions, by software disruptions, and by user interface problems. Also we can separate patterns by intention such as malware (with unintentional patterns, the rest, all grouped as Victimware). In this presentation we only consider network traces as a subtype of software traces.

Meta-patterns:
http://www.dumpanalysis.org/blog/index.php/2012/06/09/patterns-of-software-diagnostics-part-1/

Software Log:
http://www.dumpanalysis.org/blog/index.php/trace-analysis-patterns/

Memory Dump:
http://www.dumpanalysis.org/blog/index.php/crash-dump-analysis-patterns/

Network Trace:
http://www.dumpanalysis.org/blog/index.php/2012/07/19/network-trace-analysis-patterns-part-1/

Problem Description:
http://www.dumpanalysis.org/blog/index.php/2012/03/11/software-problem-description-patterns-part-1/

Software Disruption:
http://www.dumpanalysis.org/blog/index.php/2013/01/12/software-disruption-patterns-part-1/

UI Problem:
http://www.dumpanalysis.org/blog/index.php/user-interface-problem-analysis-patterns/

Malware:
http://www.dumpanalysis.org/blog/index.php/malware-analysis-patterns/

Traces and Logs

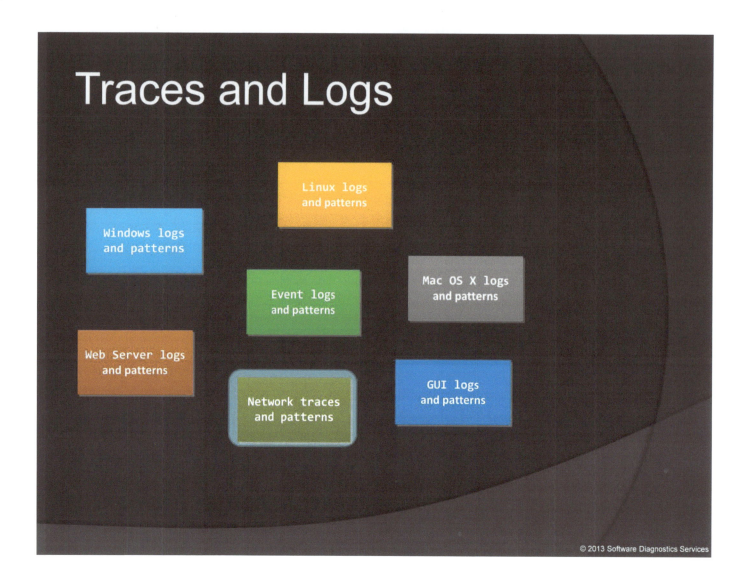

Software diagnostics analyses various software traces and logs. There are so many of them with different formats, OS and product specific information.

Trace and Log Patterns

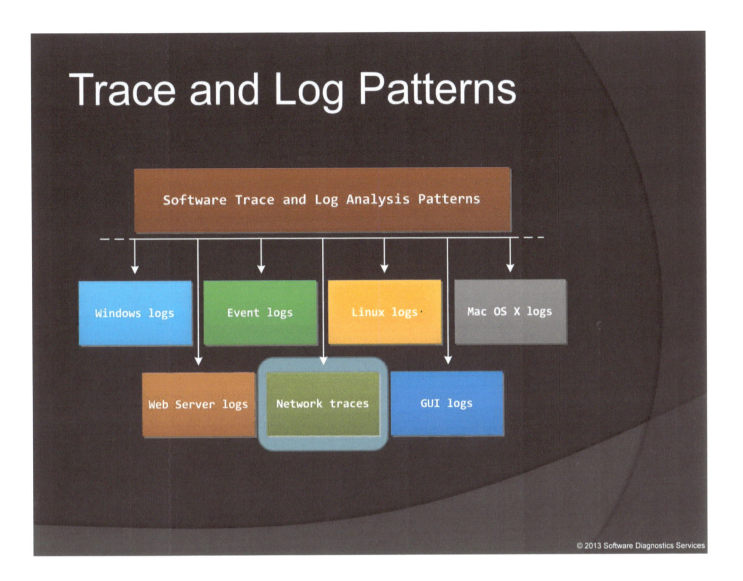

A unifying approach was needed for a pattern catalog. The needed solution would use the common structure of all these logs and associated patterns. Initially we didn't consider network traces and added them as afterthought to make sense of them. Fortunately, software trace and log analysis patterns are applicable to network trace analysis because network traces can be considered as software narratives.

Software Narrative

A temporal sequence of events related to software execution.

The analysis of software narratives uses narratology, the discipline that studies various narrative forms such as stories, novels, chronicles, dialogues, because all these narratives have the same unified structure such as events ordered by time.

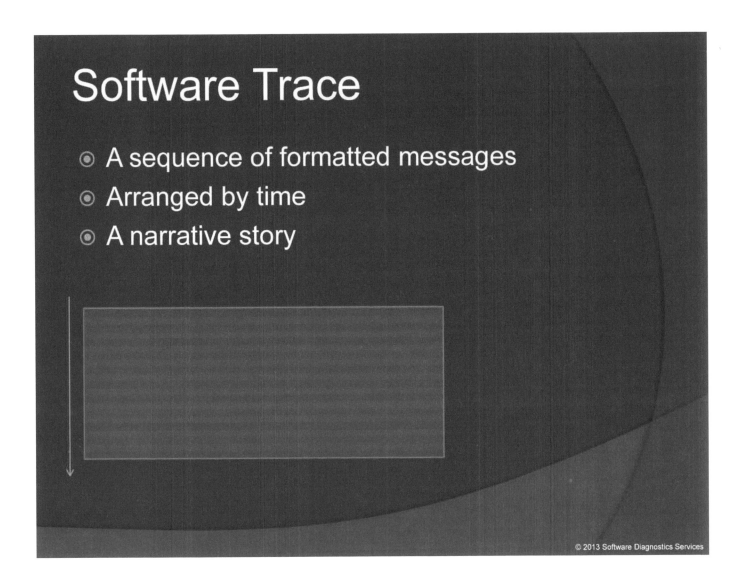

For our purposes a software trace is just a sequence of formatted messages sent from running software, for example, an event log or intercepted and formatted API requests such as a log from Process Monitor tool or a network trace. They are usually arranged by time and can be considered as a software narrative story.

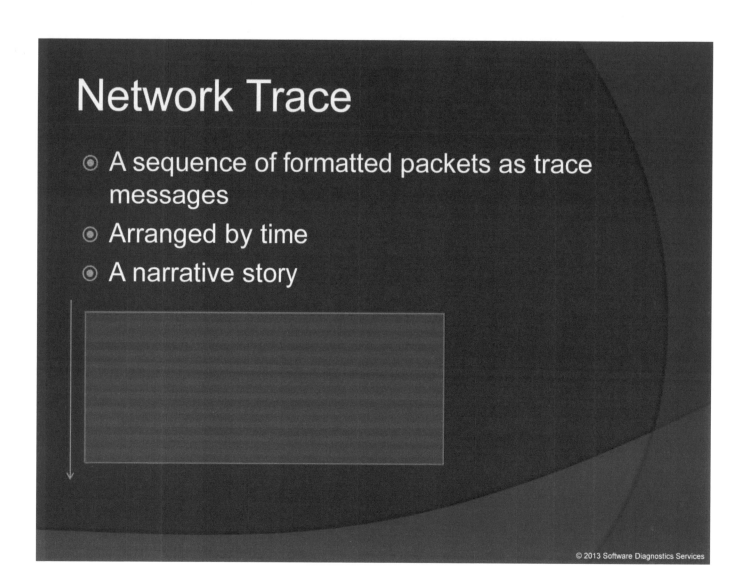

Network Trace

- A sequence of formatted packets as trace messages
- Arranged by time
- A narrative story

Network trace analysis is done on a packet level and packets can be considered as trace messages too. We analyze a network trace for any structural and behavioral patterns from a pattern catalogue.

Network Trace Analysis

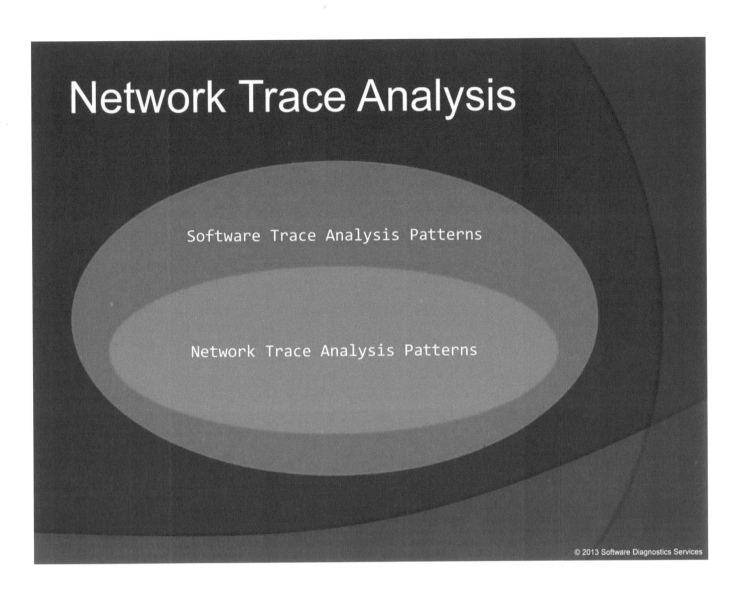

By network trace analysis patterns we consider a subset of software trace and log analysis patterns because they all have the same underlying narratological structure.

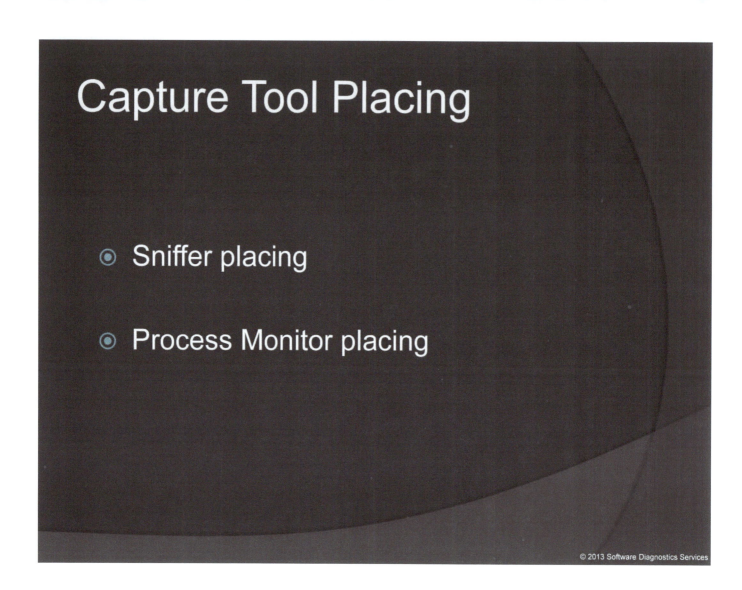

There are more similarities with a software trace analysis. For example, in a distributed environment we need to plan on what computers we should do our tracing.

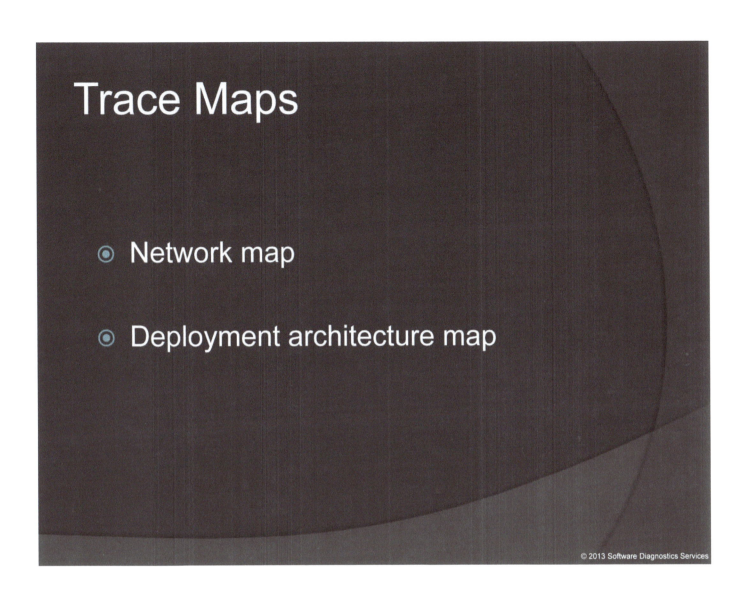

The same goes for network and product deployment diagrams. It's good to have them before troubleshooting.

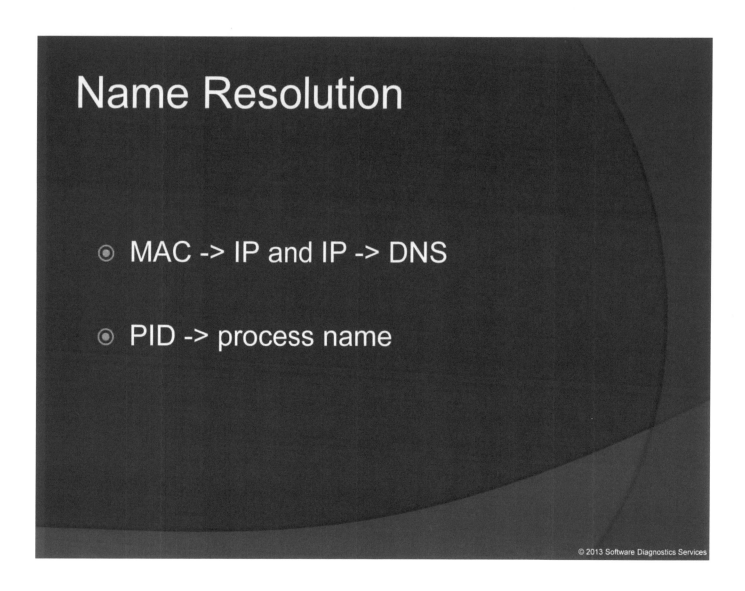

There are also parallels for better trace presentation such as converting data to human readable formats with added semantics. Presentation or trace representation is also a part of software narratology and narratology in general as we can see on the following slide I borrowed from the previous Software Narratology presentation.

Trace Presentation

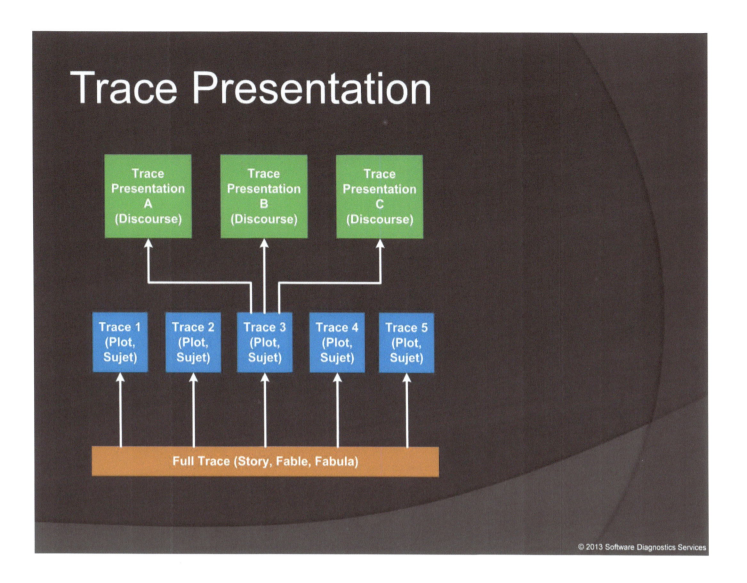

The events of the whole full story (also called a fable or fabula) can be rearranged in numerous ways to create various plots (with suspention as in fiction thrillers) also called sujets. Before or during network capture the tracing of certain packets can be switched off or on. When we analyze network traces we apply certain display filters in order to reduce their size. So we get different network plots or sujects from the possible full network story or fabula. But every individual plot can be presented differently, for example, in a novel or a poem, and even in a movie. The same goes for network software stories as well.

Minimal Trace Graphs

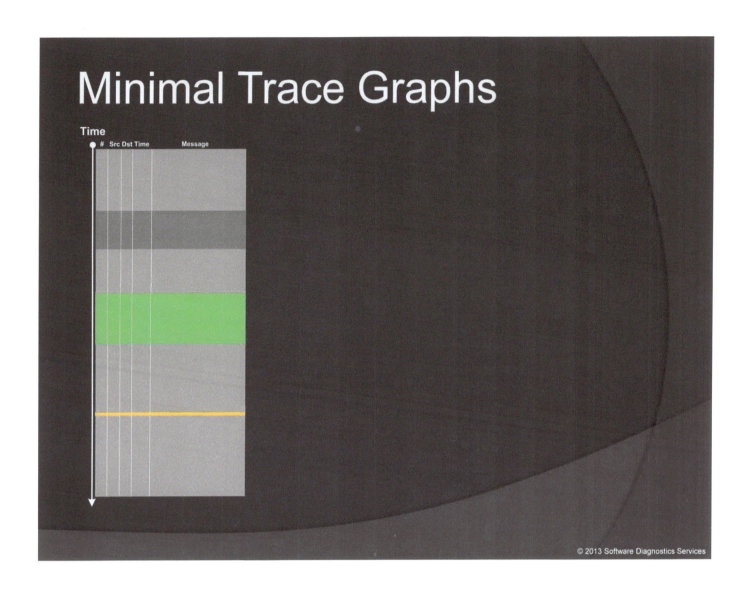

In order to illustrate network trace analysis patterns graphically we use the simplified abstracted pictorial representation of a typical software log. It has all essential features such as message number, time, endpoints and packet data itself.

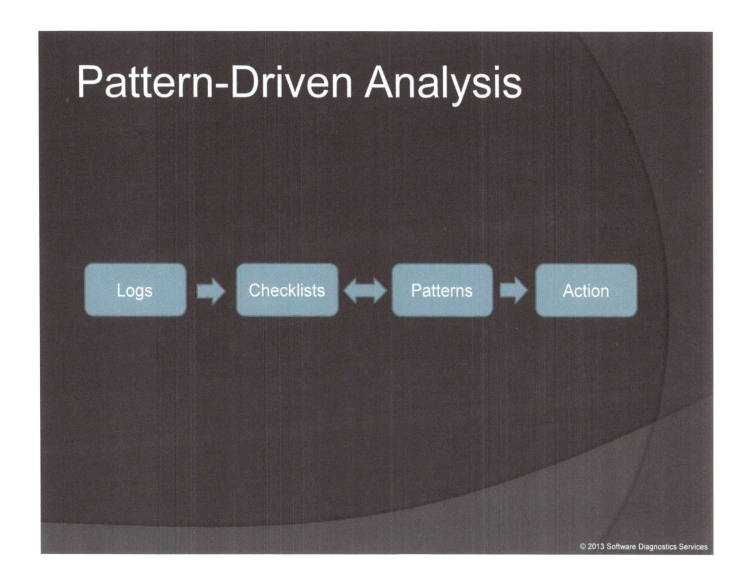

A few words about logs, checklists, and patterns. You probably have seen the same diagram in previous webinars and trainings. This is an essential feature of pattern-driven software diagnostics. Software trace analysis is usually an analysis of a formatted text for the presence of patterns. Here checklists can be very useful.

Pattern-Based Analysis

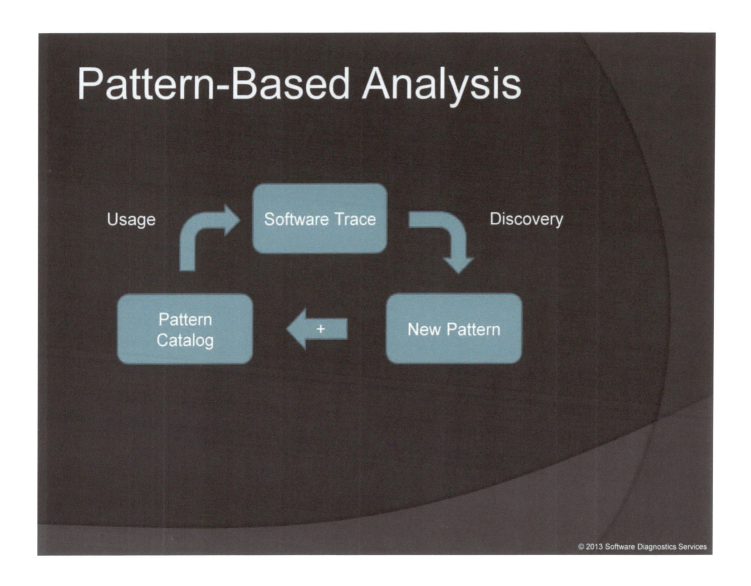

Pattern catalogs are rarely fixed. New patterns are constantly discerned or refined. For example, while preparing this webinar I found yet another missing pattern for network conversations and added it to the trace analysis pattern catalog. It became useful not only for network trace analysis but also for window message logs and multi-computer traces.

Pattern Classification

- Vocabulary
- Error
- Trace as a Whole
- Large Scale
- Activity
- Message
- Block
- Trace Set

Recently all software trace and log analysis patterns (which are now numbered more than 70 at the time of this writing) were classified into several categories. Vocabulary category consists of patterns related to problem description. Error category covers general error distribution patterns. This classification also considers traces as wholes, their large scale structure, activity patterns, patterns related to individual trace message structure, patterns related to collection of messages (the so called blocks) and finally patterns related to several traces and logs as a collection of artifacts from a software incident. Because network trace analysis is only a part of general software diagnostics and we just started exploring network narratives we selected only a few patterns from these categories as relevant to illustrate our software narratological approach.

Reference and Course

- Catalog from Software Diagnostics Library

  Software Trace Analysis Patterns

- Free reference graphical slides

  Accelerated-Windows-Software-Trace-Analysis-Public.pdf

- Training course*

  Accelerated Windows Software Trace Analysis

  * Available as a full color paperback book, PDF book, on SkillsSoft Books 24x7. Recording is available for all book formats

  © 2013 Software Diagnostics Services

Most patterns are very intuitive if you analyse network traces and software logs in general. Here I provided a few links for general software trace and log analysis used as a foundation for pattern-oriented network trace analysis. After you download a presentation you can follow these links.

Software Trace Analysis Patterns:
http://www.dumpanalysis.org/blog/index.php/trace-analysis-patterns/

Free reference graphical slides:
http://www.patterndiagnostics.com/Training/Accelerated-Windows-Software-Trace-Analysis-Public.pdf

Training course:
http://www.patterndiagnostics.com/accelerated-software-trace-analysis

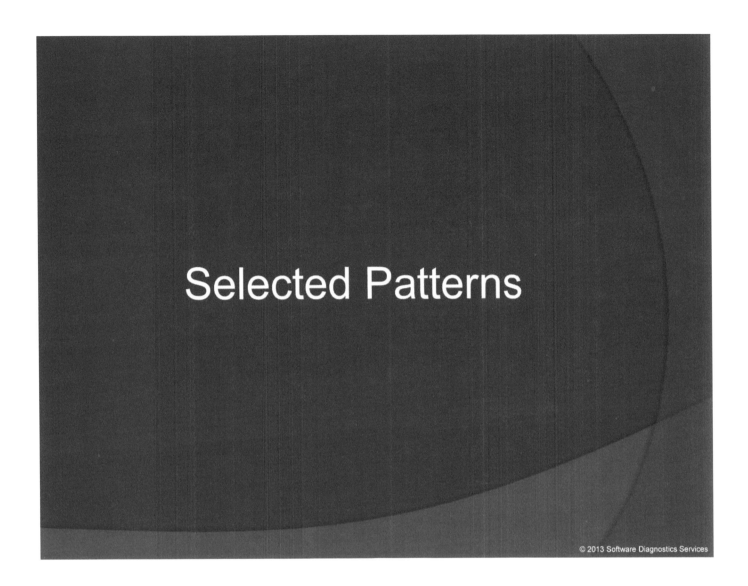

Now I present a few selected patterns with diagrams.

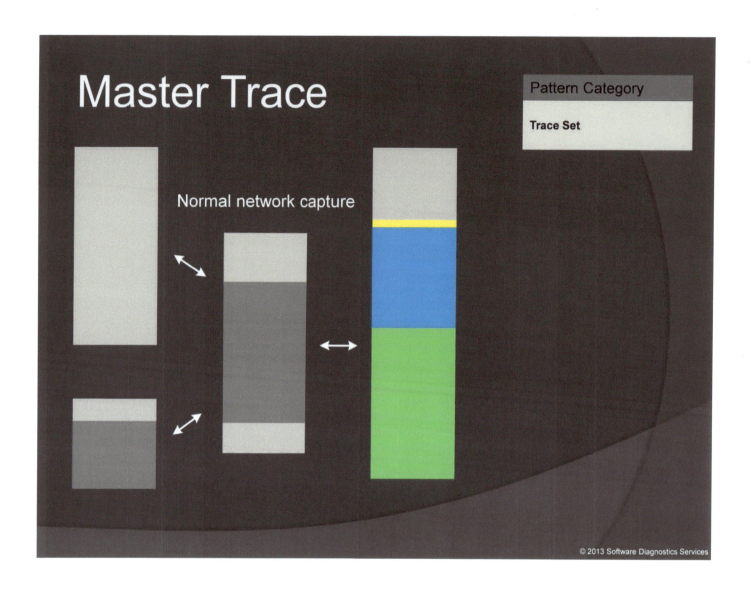

When reading and analyzing network traces and logs we always compare them to a **Master Trace** which is a standard or normal network capture.

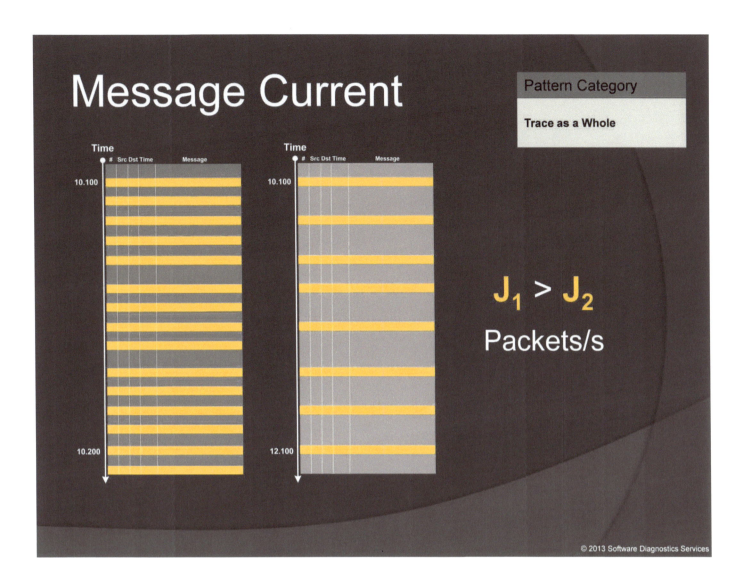

Message Current (also called Statement Current) is the number of messages per unit of time. This is similar to velosity, first-order derivative. A trace can also be partitioned into **Activity Regions** with different currents and current can also be measured between significant trace events.

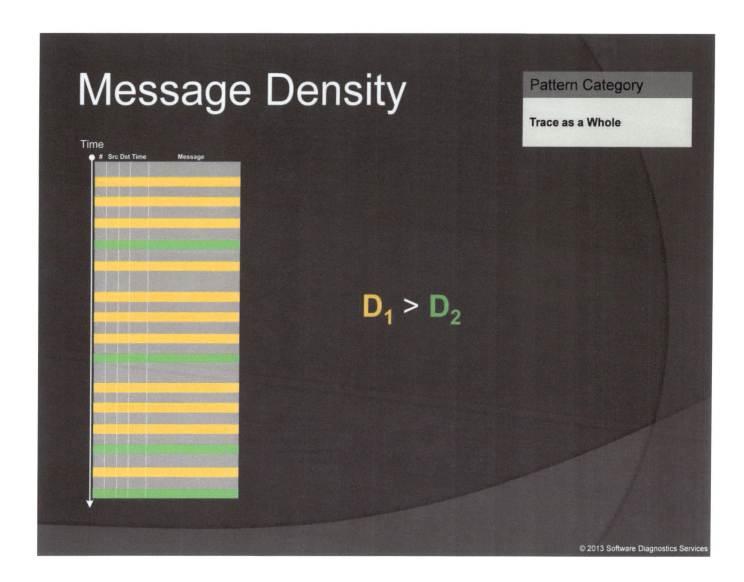

The statement or message density is simply the ratio of the number of occurrences of the specific trace statement (message) in the trace to the total number of all different recorded messages.

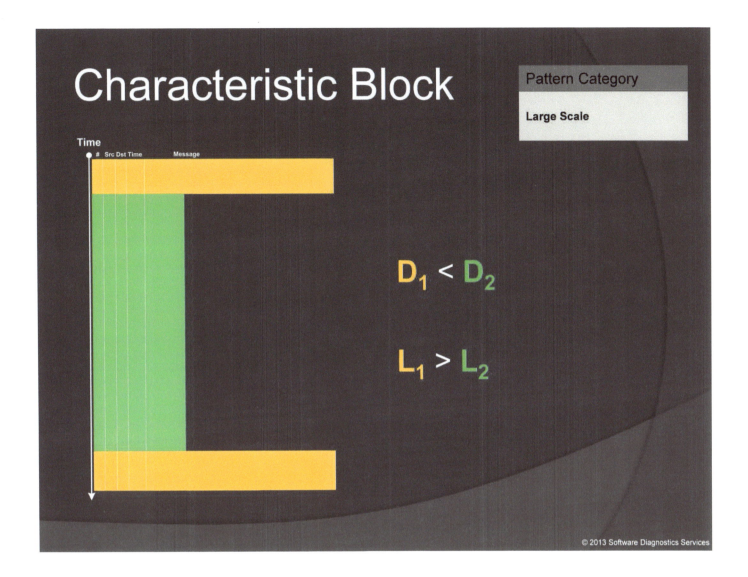

Message part can be variable and despite less density certain endpoints may generate more byte traffic. The full name of this pattern is **Characteristic Message Block** and originally it was devised for irregularities of formatting and here payload length may serve well but generally any characteristic function can be applied.

Example

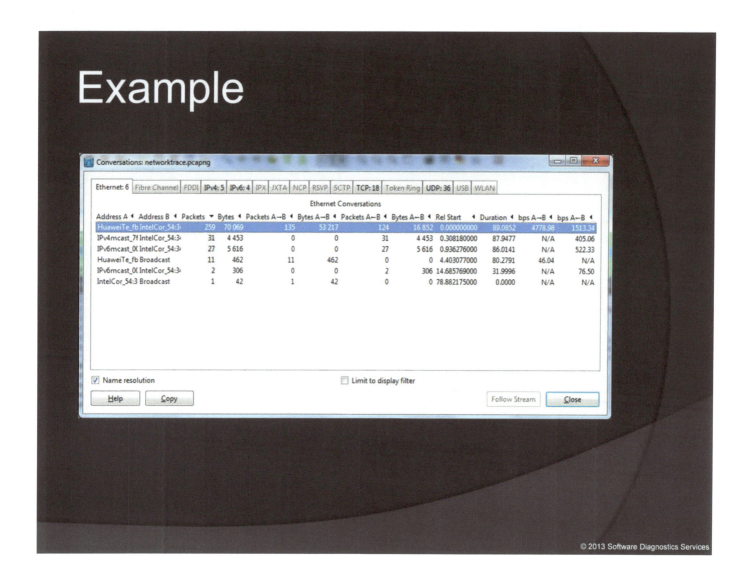

All the latter patterns can be seen in Conversations dialog in Wireshark.

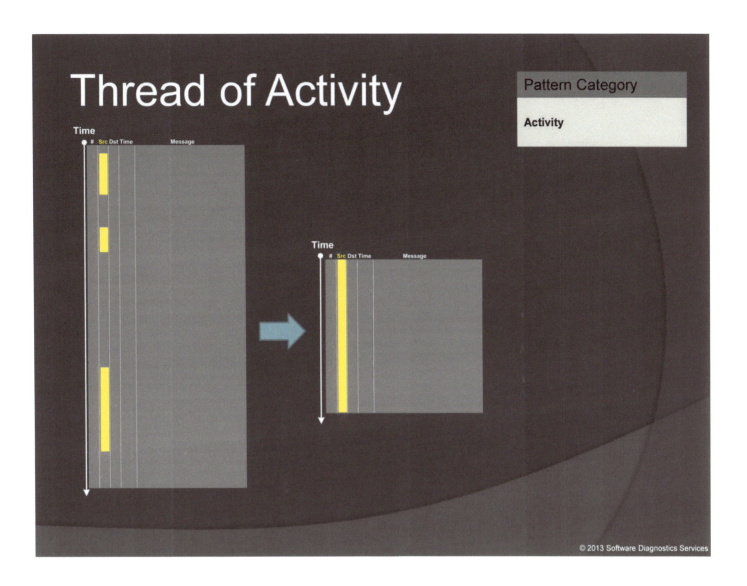

In software trace analysis **Thread of Activity** pattern usually means trace messages associated with the particular Thread ID. Usually when we see an error indication or some interesting message we select its current thread and investigate what happened in this process and thread before. By looking at threads we can also spot discontinuities. In network trace analysis we can select a source as a thread, for example.

Adjoint Thread

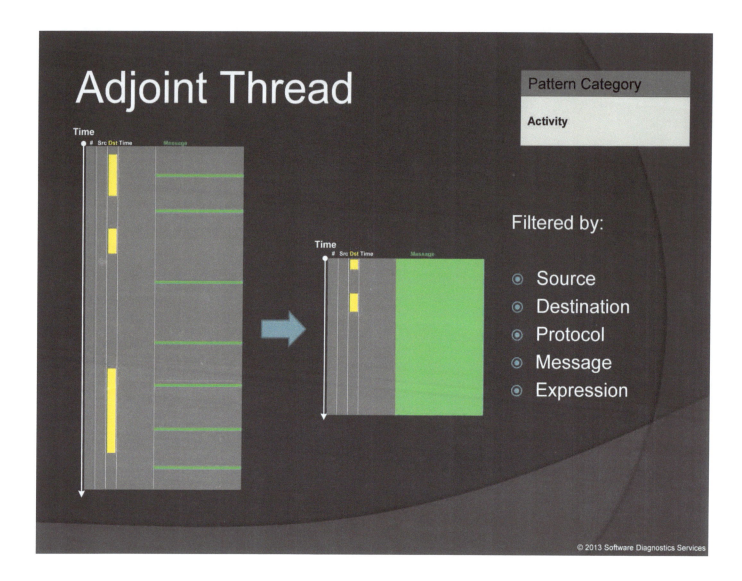

If a thread is a linear ordered flow of activities associated with particular Thread ID or Source as seen from trace message perspective through time we can also extend this flow concept and consider a linear flow of activities associated with some other parameter such as Destination, Protocol, Message or some expression. Such trace messages may have different Thread IDs or sources associated with them but also some chosen constant parameter or column value in a trace viewing tool. The name **adjoint** comes from the fact that in threads of activity Thread ID or Source stays the same but other message attributes vary but in adjoint threads we have the opposite.

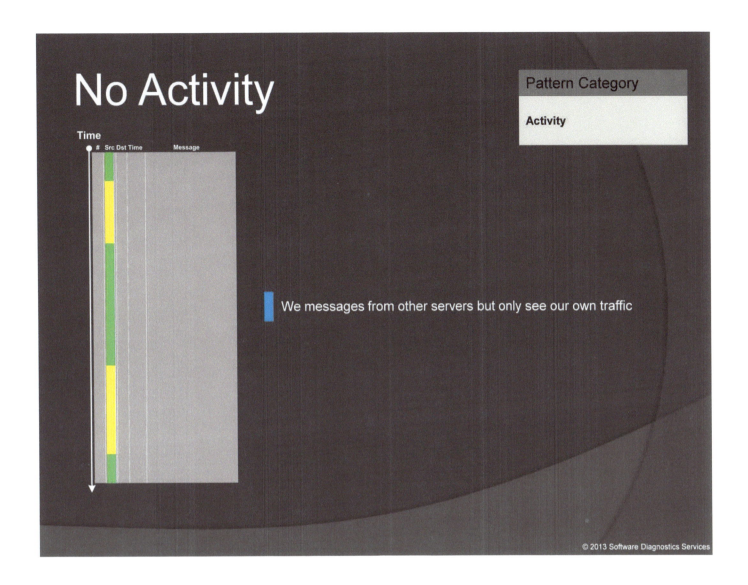

No Activity is an obvious pattern when we don't see any expected trace messages. It could also be the case of endpoints or protocols not selected for tracing. It is a limit of the next pattern called **Discontinuity**.

Discontinuity

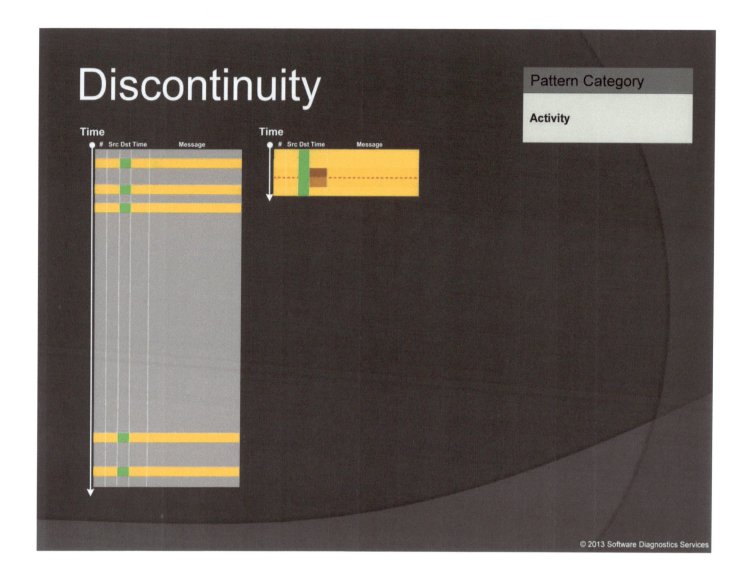

This pattern is about delays. When we select **Thread of Activity** or **Adjoint Thread of Activity** we see such delays better.

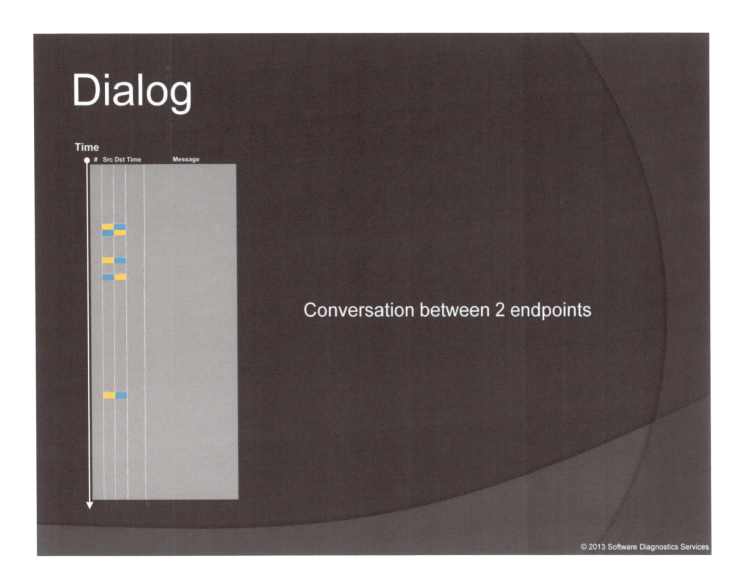

Dialogue is an important pattern especially in network trace analysis. It usually involves a message source, a different message target (although both can be the same) and some alternation between them as shown on this abstract trace diagram. This pattern was added recently and has not yet been classified.

Significant Event

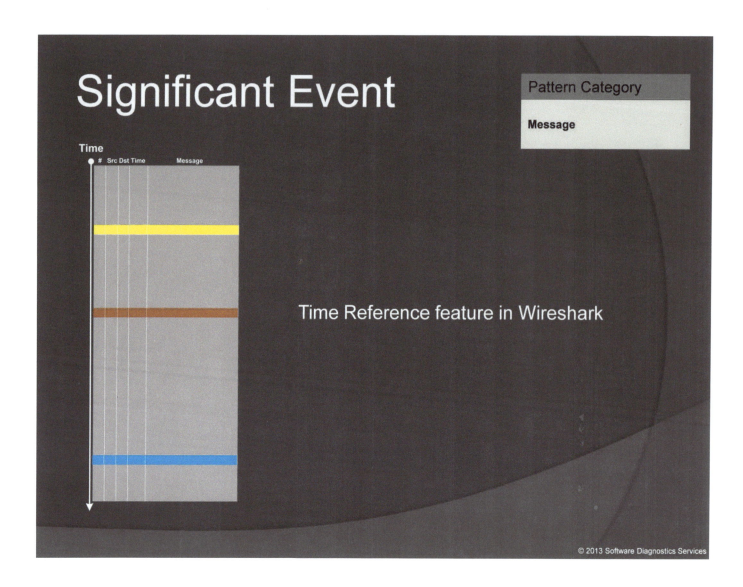

Time Reference feature in Wireshark

When looking at a network trace and doing search for or just scrolling certain messages have our attention immediately. We call them **Significant Events**. The start of a trace and the end of it are trivial significant events and are used in deciding whether the trace is **Circular**, and also in determining the trace recording interval (**Time Delta** pattern) or its average **Message Current**. Some significant messages can be used as a time reference too.

Marked Messages

Annotated messages:

```
session initialization [+]
session tear-off [-]
port A activity [+]
port B activity [-]
protocol C used [-]
address D used [-]
```

Marked Packets
feature in Wireshark

[+] activity is present in a trace
[-] activity is undetected or not present

This pattern groups trace messages based on having some feature or property. For example, marked messages may point to some network activity and therefore may help in troubleshooting and debugging. Unmarked messages include all other messages that don't say anything about such activities (although may include messages pointing to such activities indirectly we unaware of) or messages that say explicitly that no such activity has occurred. We can annotate any trace or log after analysis to compare it with a **Master Trace** pattern (which is a normal expected network trace). Sometimes a non-present activity can be a marked activity corresponding to all inclusive unmarked present activity (for example, **No Activity** pattern). Some tools such as Wireshark allow you to mark specific trace messages to help in analysis.

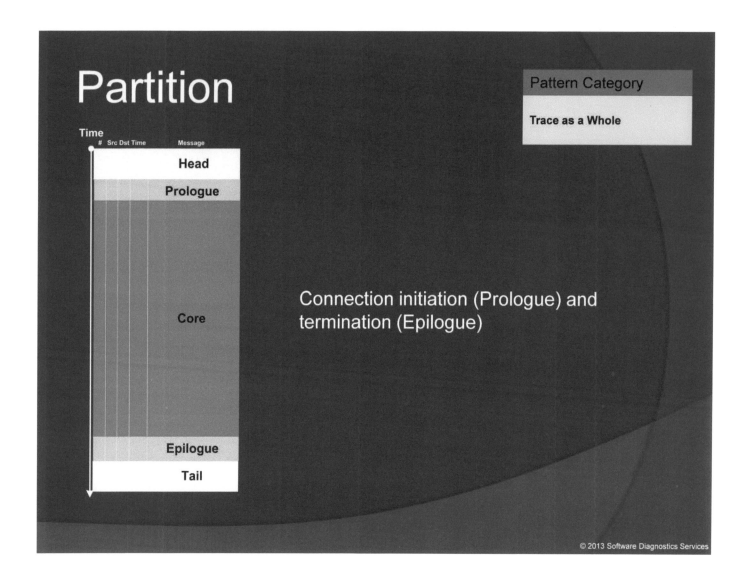

Here we introduce a software narratological (like a software story) partitioning of a network trace into **Head**, **Prologue**, **Core**, **Epilogue** and **Tail** segments. Some elements such as **Head** and **Tail** may be optional and combined with **Prologue** and **Epilogue**. This is useful for comparative network trace analysis. Please note that such partitioning can be done for any filtered trace such as **Adjoint Thread of Activity**.

Inter-Correlation

⊙ Several packet sniffers at once

⊙ Internal and external views

Process Monitor log + network trace

This pattern involves several traces from possibly different network trace tools recorded (most commonly) at the same time or during an overlapping time interval or a combination of a network trace with some other trace or log such as from Process Monitor. The purpose of using different tracing tools is to cover events more completely.

Circular Trace

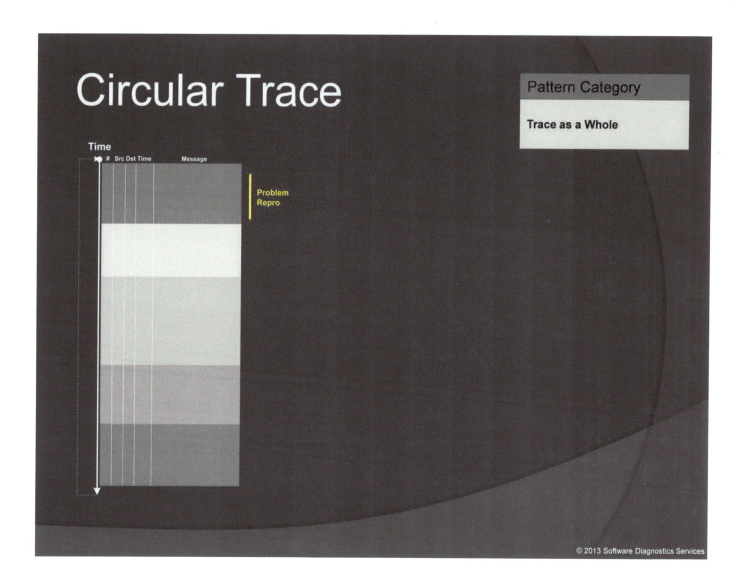

One of common problems with tracing are rare and non-reproducible incidents. If the amount of traffic is small per second it is possible to record events for hours or days. However if we need to trace all communication as to do filtering later then trace files can grow uncontrollable. Some tools enable circular tracing and after reaching particular file size the tracing stream overwrites older messages.

Split Trace

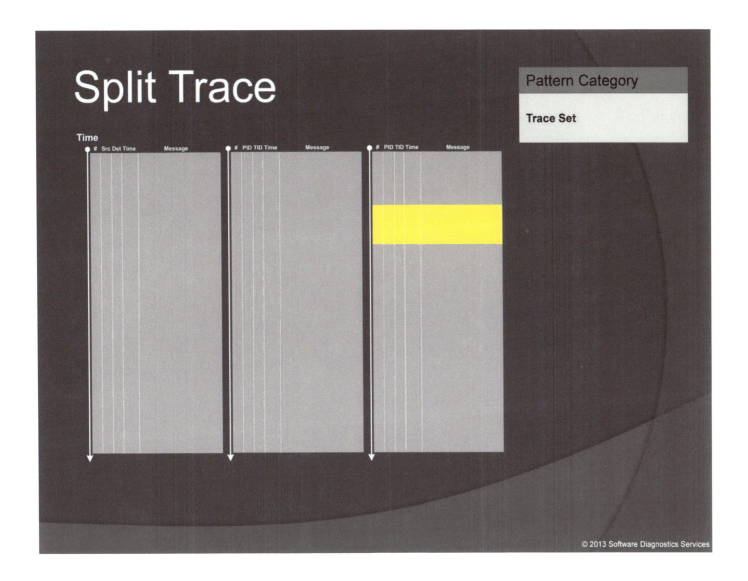

Some network tracing tools such as Wireshark have an option to split network traces into several files during long capture. Although this should be done judiciously it is really necessary sometimes.

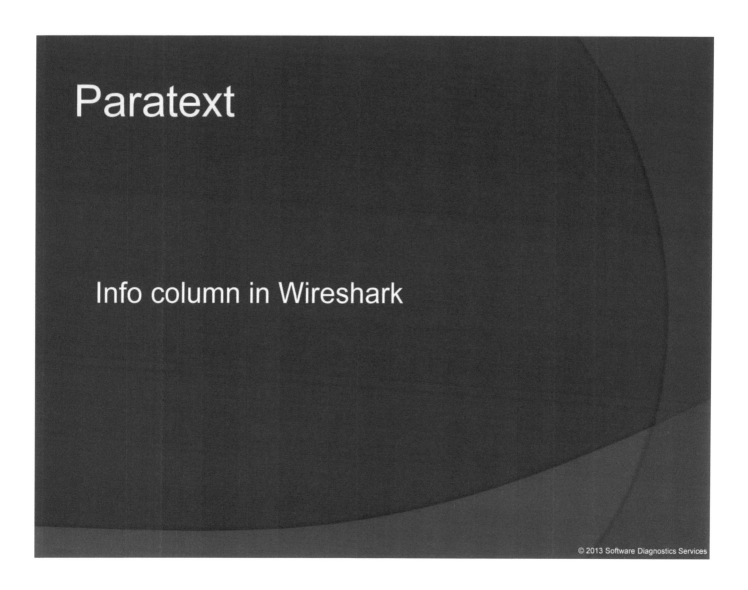

Additional useful concept from narratology is a concept of a paratext. This is additional information about a text useful for its interpretation such as a book cover, an introduction from an editor, notes or the list of other referenced texts. This is not a pattern yet and will be added to the catalogue soon.

Frames

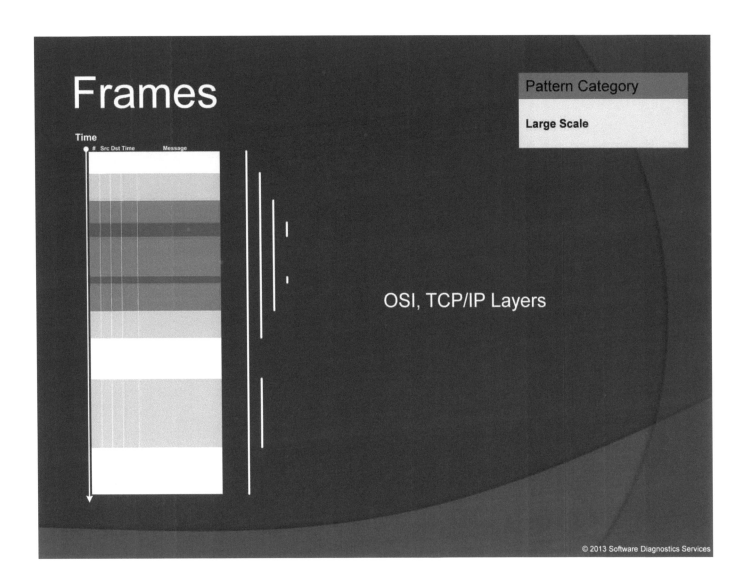

Frames pattern can describe various protocol layers.

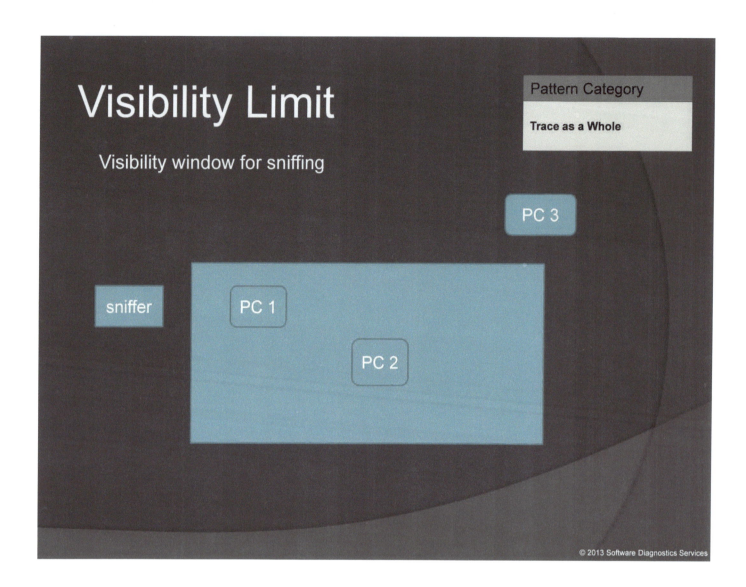

Sometimes due to network configuration or sniffer placement some computers will be excluded and their traffic will not be seen in a trace. In the context of a general software trace **Visibility Tracing** pattern means impossibility of logging some functionality, for example, before the tracing subsystem or service starts.

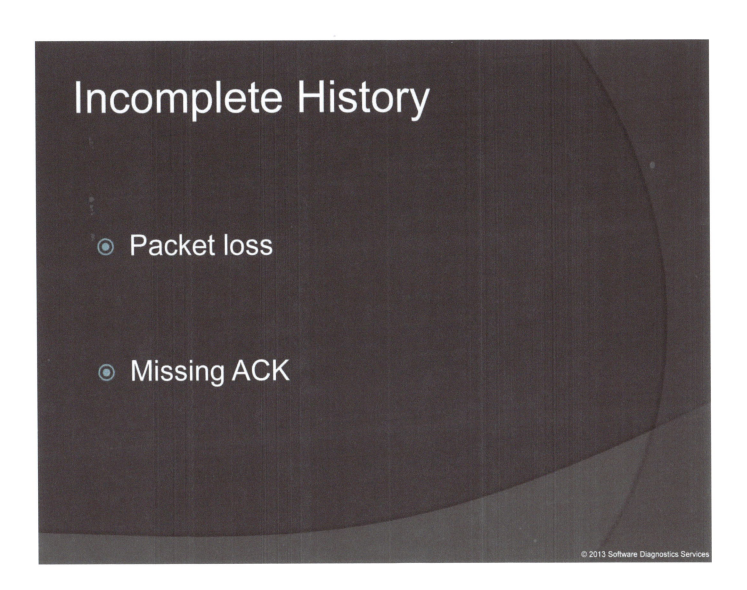

Due to a packet loss we may have an incomplete tracing history. Missing responses or acknowledgements are also covered by this pattern.

Possible New Patterns

- Full Trace (promiscuous mode)

- Embedded Message (PDU chain, protocol data unit, packet)

- Ordered Message (TCP/IP sequence numbers)

- Illegal Message (sniffed with illegally obtained privileges)

- Dual Trace (in / out, duplex)

On this slide we list an incomplete list of some possible patterns we plan to evaluate and add in the future to our trace analysis pattern catalogue.

Further Reading

- Practical Packet Analysis, 2nd edition, by Chris Sanders

- Software Diagnostics Institute

- Memory Dump Analysis Anthology: Volumes 3, 4, 5, 6, …
  Volume 7 is in preparation (July, 2013)

- Introduction to Software Narratology

- Malware Narratives

So we have covered a few selected patterns. Here are some links for further reading. On top we list a wonderful book especially useful for beginners in network trace analysis. The rest are links including to 2 other presentations on software trace analysis: *Introduction to Software Narratology* and *Malware Narratives*.

Software Diagnostics Institute:

http://www.dumpanalysis.org

Memory Dump Analysis Anthology volumes:

http://www.patterndiagnostics.com/ultimate-memory-analysis-reference

Introduction to Software Narratology:

http://www.patterndiagnostics.com/Introduction-Software-Narratology-materials

Malware Narratives:

http://www.patterndiagnostics.com/malware-narratives-materials

What's Next?

- Accelerated Network Trace Analysis

- Generative Software Narratology

- Pattern-Oriented Hardware Signal Analysis

The next application of software narratology we plan is hardware analysis. We also plan to extend software narratology to its generative form to include a layer of source code. We also plan training similar to *Accelerated Windows Software Trace Analysis* we developed last year. It is called *Accelerated Network Trace Analysis* and will have hands-on exercises for Wireshark and Network Monitor or possibly its successor Message Analyzer if it is released by that time. This training will also cover all applicable trace analysis patterns from our catalogue.

Generative Software Narratology:
http://www.patterndiagnostics.com/introduction-generative-software-narratology